LOVE LAYOFF

HR STRATEGIES FOR NAVIGATING
RELATIONSHIP CLOSURE

NAKISHA GREGORY
JAHNNI ALLEN

Dear Reader,

This book is not just a collection of words on paper—it's a heartfelt invitation to embark on a transformative journey of healing, growth, and self-discovery. For every silent tear you've shed and every moment of uncertainty you've faced, know that you are not alone. We stand with you, hand in hand, as fellow travelers on this path toward healing and renewal.

As you turn these pages, may you find solace in knowing that your struggles are not vain. Each trial and setback has sculpted you into the resilient soul you are today. From the depths of despair emerges an unwavering spirit that refuses to be defined by heartbreak but instead embraces it as a catalyst for growth.

Your story is a vibrant thread in the tapestry of life—a testament to your courage, strength, and unyielding determination. We've condensed our message to ensure each word carries the weight of our collective empathy and encouragement. Let these pages be a beacon of hope, guiding you through the darkest nights toward the dawn of a new day.

Consider Virginia, who found herself adrift in a sea of uncertainty after the end of a long-term relationship. Through the use of this book and introspection and self-discovery, she unearthed hidden reservoirs of strength and resilience she never knew she possessed. Her journey is a testament to the transformative power of healing and growth.

As you navigate these pages, we invite you to reflect deeply. What lessons can you glean from your past experiences? What aspirations stir within your heart, waiting to be realized? Take a moment to set intentions for your journey— envision your desired life and take the necessary steps to manifest it into reality.

Thank you for entrusting us with your story, struggles, and triumphs. Your courage inspires us, your resilience humbles us, and your presence enriches our lives in ways words cannot express. Together, let us embark on this transformative journey with open hearts and minds, knowing that the best is yet to come.

With heartfelt gratitude and unwavering support,

Nakisha J. Gregory and Jahnni Allen

TABLE OF CONTENTS

ABOUT THE AUTHORS

Nakisha J. Gregory is an International Best-Selling Author and acclaimed Relationship Marketing Strategist specializing in personal development and navigating relationship closures. Her background is enriched by diverse experiences in communication, psychology, and marketing, and she brings a unique blend of expertise and compassion to her work.

Throughout her career, Nakisha has dedicated herself to understanding the complexities of human connection, both in personal and professional contexts. Her moniker, "The Madam Cupid of Relationship Marketing," reflects her ability to merge marketing savvy with deep insights into the dynamics of personal relationships.

Beyond her professional achievements, Nakisha fervently advocates for self-care and mental health. She hosts workshops and seminars aimed at helping individuals rediscover their self-worth and navigate the path to personal fulfillment post-breakup. Nakisha's writing, characterized by its insightfulness and empathy, guides countless individuals seeking to rebuild their lives with confidence and purpose.

Nakisha's influence extends beyond her published works. Through her engaging social media presence and contributions to various online platforms, she fosters a community of support and learning. Her approachable demeanor and compassionate nature make her a trusted figure for those seeking advice on love, loss, and the journey back to self-love.

As a lifelong learner and seeker of wisdom in human relationships, Nakisha continues to explore new ways to support individuals in their quest for happiness and fulfillment. Her upcoming projects promise to further her mission of helping people around the globe to love deeply, heal fully, and embrace the possibilities of new beginnings.

Jahnni Allen is a seasoned professional in Employee Relations with over a decade of experience. Her career has been dedicated to creating empathetic, understanding, and resilient work environments, showcasing her expertise in enhancing employee wellness and organizational culture across various sectors. Jahnni holds a Positive Psychology Certification, which complements her deep understanding of human psychology and workplace dynamics.

Driven by a deep interest in human psychology and workplace dynamics, Jahnni focuses on understanding how personal life events, particularly relationship closures, can impact professional performance and workplace morale. Her background spans healthcare, public transportation, and corporate settings, giving her a broad perspective on the interplay between personal well-being and professional success.

As an Employee Relations Partner, Jahnni has been instrumental in developing initiatives that significantly improve employee satisfaction, engagement, and mental health. Her efforts in administering comprehensive benefit plans, driving employee engagement initiatives, and overseeing wellness programs have made a substantial impact on the organizations she has worked with.

In her collaboration on "Love Layoff," Jahnni leverages her extensive experience to explore how employee relations principles can be aptly applied to personal relationship closures. Her insights into the similarities between corporate exit interviews and personal relationship endings provide a structured and insightful approach to managing breakups, emphasizing personal growth.

Jahnni's contribution to this book extends beyond her professional insight; her compassionate understanding of emotional challenges post-breakup enriches the narrative. She underscores the critical role of support systems and the importance of self-care, guiding readers through emotional liberation and professional renewal.

As a respected figure in employee relations and a trusted advisor on achieving personal and professional well-being, Jahnni's collaboration with Nakisha J. Gregory on "Love Layoff" highlights her dedication to helping others navigate the challenges of relationship endings, fostering resilience, balance, and happiness in every aspect of life.

INTRODUCTION

In the intricate dance of relationships, the conclusion often leaves us in a labyrinth of emotions, questioning, and seeking. Like a beacon of light in that labyrinth, the "Love Layoff" illuminates paths not just out of heartache but through it, transforming pain into strength and clarity. Imagine standing at the crossroads of a breakup, unsure of which direction to take next. "Love Layoff" isn't just a map; it's a trusted guide, offering navigation through the storm of emotions and into calmer waters.

This guide doesn't merely offer solace; it equips you with a unique blend of strategies inspired by the professional world's exit interview process. Here, you're invited to undertake a journey of deep personal introspection, turning the end of a relationship into a powerful catalyst for individual and emotional healing. Much like the closure process in the corporate world, "Love Layoff" provides a structured approach to bidding farewell to the past while embracing the promise of new beginnings.

Designed to be more than a guide, "Love Layoff" is a steadfast companion as you navigate the complexities of ending a chapter in your life. It offers understanding and actionable steps for moving forward and instills profound empowerment. This book aims to bridge the gap between personal upheaval and professional resilience through thoughtful strategies and exercises, fostering a harmonious balance that nurtures both heart and career.

As you delve into these pages, you'll be introduced to a holistic approach to healing. This approach acknowledges personal relationships' profound impact on all our lives, including our work. By adopting techniques typically reserved for professional development and applying them to our individual lives, "Love Layoff" creates a comprehensive framework for recovery and growth. It's a testament to the belief that every ending promises a new beginning, and every heartache carries the potential for profound transformation and renewal.

Whether you're in the throes of a recent breakup or still untangling the emotional aftermath of a past relationship, "Love Layoff" offers you the tools, insights, and encouragement needed to embark on a journey toward healing, self-discovery, and ultimately, a renewed optimism in love and life. Prepare to step into a future where your emotional well-being is prioritized, and you're fully equipped to navigate the complexities of relationships with grace, resilience, and a heart ready for new adventures.

1

HEALING AND LETTING GO: A CLOSURE PERFORMANCE REVIEW

This chapter introduces the concept of a "Closure Performance Review," a structured approach to releasing resentment that mirrors professional performance evaluations. This innovative method guides readers through emotional introspection, understanding, and release, offering a holistic path to healing influenced by personal and professional relationship dynamics. Integrating techniques typically reserved for the workplace—such as objective assessments and structured feedback—into personal emotional recovery, the Closure Performance Review encourages a thorough examination of past relationships and personal interactions. This method helps identify and process underlying feelings of resentment. It promotes a deeper understanding of personal behavioral patterns and triggers. The aim is to transform negative emotions into constructive insights, empowering readers to achieve emotional clarity and strengthen emotional resilience. By applying a systematic approach to personal closure, similar to how one might analyze and learn from a professional project, individuals are better equipped to foster healthier relationships and achieve personal growth.

Understanding the Impact of Resentment

Resentment can anchor us to past hurts, obstructing our emotional and personal development. Recognizing its toll on our well-being is crucial to initiating healing. This negative emotion can linger subconsciously, coloring our perceptions and reactions in ways that might not be immediately apparent, leading to a cycle of negativity that impacts our emotional health, relationships, and overall happiness. To break free from this cycle, it is essential to delve deep into the sources of resentment, examining specific incidents or interactions and broader patterns of behavior and expectations that may contribute to these feelings.

- Exercise: Reflect on how resentment has shaped your emotions, relationships, and happiness. Consider its roots and the breadth of its impact. Answer the following questions to guide your reflection, writing down your responses to help clarify your thoughts and feelings:

1. What specific events trigger my resentment?

   - Answer: _____

_____

_____

2. How does this feeling manifest in my interactions with others?

   - Answer: _____

_____

3. What physical or emotional signs indicate that I am holding onto resentment?

- Answer: _____

_____

_____

This structured approach not only helps you acknowledge the presence of resentment but also aids in understanding its triggers and effects. By comprehensively addressing these questions, you can begin to identify the steps needed to release these feelings and move towards a more fulfilling and emotionally healthy life.

Broadened Strategies for Letting Go of Resentment

1. Acknowledging Your Feelings: Directly confront resentment by recognizing and accepting your emotions without judgment. This self-awareness is pivotal for forward movement. Allow yourself to experience your emotions, providing a foundation for healing fully.

2. Empathy Mapping: Gain insight into the other person's perspective. This doesn't excuse their behavior but helps understand motivations, offering a pathway to empathy. Attempting to see situations from the other person's point of view can decrease personal biases and misunderstandings that fuel resentment.

3. Expressive Writing: Craft a letter detailing your feelings toward the person you resent. This act is a cathartic release, even if the

letter is never sent. Arranging your emotions can help you process and often release them.

4. Forgiveness Focus: Redirect your energy toward forgiveness, which benefits you more than anyone else. Forgiveness can liberate you from resentment, freeing you from the negative emotional burden and allowing you to move forward.

5. Boundary Reinforcement: Use this newfound understanding to define healthier boundaries in future interactions, safeguarding your emotional space. Clear boundaries help prevent similar situations from occurring, protecting your emotional well-being.

6. Gratitude Practice: Shift your focus from negative to positive by cultivating gratitude. Recognize the good in your life, counterbalancing the bitterness of resentment. This practice can shift your mindset from what you lack to what you possess, fostering positive emotions.

7. Self-Care Commitment: Engage in activities that uplift your spirit, affirm your self-worth, and aid healing. This could include physical activities, hobbies, social interactions, or anything else that makes you feel good about yourself and your life.

Enhanced Interactive Exercise: Your Performance Review

Dedicate time for a reflective session, applying the chapter's strategies to conduct a thorough Closure Performance Review. Explore the nuances of the relationship or situation causing resentment with guided questions for a richer emotional understanding:

1. What revelations about myself have emerged from this situation?

   - Answer: _____

_____

_____

2. How can I incorporate these insights to enhance my emotional well-being and future connections?

   - Answer: _____

_____

_____

3. In what ways have I emerged more resilient or insightful?

   - Answer: _____

_____

_____

This exercise facilitates a deeper understanding of your emotions and encourages a proactive approach to personal growth. By integrating the insights from this review, you can develop strategies that foster resilience, leading to a more balanced and fulfilling emotional life.

Real-Life Scenario and Author Insights

Real-World Scenario: Consider the case of Emma, a marketing professional who recently went through a tough breakup. Using the Closure Performance Review, she realized that her resentment stemmed from the breakup, unmet expectations, and a lack of communication, which plagued her professional relationships. Emma addressed these feelings through Empathy Mapping and Expressive Writing exercises, leading her to a deeper understanding of her personal and professional interactions. This process allowed Emma to articulate her needs more clearly and set healthy boundaries at work, significantly improving her recovery and professional relationships. As a result, she became more adept at managing team projects and communicating effectively with her colleagues, transforming potential conflicts into opportunities for collaboration and understanding. This holistic approach enhanced her well-being and elevated her professional capacity, proving the intertwined nature of personal insights and professional success.

Author Insights: Nakisha Gregory states, "Personal growth after a breakup can directly influence professional performance. As we learn from failed projects to improve our work strategies, understanding our role in relationship dynamics can lead to better personal decisions." Jahnni Allen reinforces this by stating, "Applying the Closure Performance Review in your personal life is like conducting a year-end review at work. It helps identify areas of strength and opportunities for growth, aligning your actions with your core values both in love and labor." This alignment enhances personal satisfaction and drives professional efficacy, illustrating how personal breakthroughs can impact broader life aspects.

- Expert Contributions: Dr. Samuel Richards, a clinical psychologist specializing in relationship dynamics, and Dr. Lisa Monroe, a therapist focusing on emotional resilience, contribute their expert perspectives. Dr. Richards explains how emotional tools designed for corporate environments are highly effective when adapted for personal use, promoting emotional intelligence and self-awareness. "These tools," he notes, "encourage individuals to reflect deeply on their interpersonal relationships and professional interactions, fostering a healthier emotional landscape." Dr. Monroe discusses the therapeutic benefits of structured introspection and emotional release, underscoring the importance of applying such strategies consistently for long-term emotional health. She adds, "Regular practice of these strategies can significantly alleviate emotional distress and enhance overall well-being, making them essential for anyone looking to maintain a healthy psychological state."

Conclusion and Deep-Dive Questions

In wrapping up, it becomes clear how integrating structured, introspective practices from our professional lives into our emotional journeys can yield profound benefits. This synthesis of work-life introspection fosters individual growth and professional development, creating a cycle of continuous improvement and deeper understanding.

Reflect on the insights and strategies discussed:

1. How have the strategies discussed influenced your view on handling personal challenges?

- Answer: _____

_____

_____

2. What steps can you take to implement the Closure Performance Review in your own life to improve both personal and professional relationships?

- Answer: _____

_____

_____

3. In what ways can enhancing emotional intelligence and self-awareness contribute to your professional success?

- Answer: _____

_____

_____

These questions are designed to help you leverage your personal experiences to enhance your professional capabilities. They underscore the interconnectedness and mutual benefits of personal development and professional growth. By exploring how personal insights and emotional growth influence your professional interactions, you can navigate workplace dynamics more effectively and cultivate more productive relationships.

As we move into Chapter 2, 'Reflecting and Learning: The Exit Interview Protocol,' we build on the foundational practices introduced in Chapter 1. This chapter delves deeper into the practical application of structured reflection techniques borrowed from professional settings to personal experiences. It mainly focuses on how structured exit interviews can facilitate closure and personal growth after a relationship ends.

In Chapter 2, we delve into how the methodology used in professional exit interviews can be adapted to process the end of personal relationships. The focus is on guiding you to conduct a personal exit interview with yourself, reviewing past relationships or significant personal experiences to extract valuable lessons and insights. This process not only aids in closure but also in understanding what values and needs are most important to you, which is crucial for future relationships and professional success,

Fundamental Concepts Covered in Chapter 2:

1. Preparation for Personal Exit Interviews: Learn how to prepare for a self-directed exit interview, setting the right environment and mindset to reflect deeply on past relationships or life events.

2. Structured Reflection Questions: Utilize a guided set of questions that mirror those used in professional exit interviews to gain clarity on what went well, what didn't, and why specific outcomes occurred in your personal life.

3. Learning from Feedback: Understand how to interpret and learn from your emotional and behavioral patterns, just as you would analyze feedback in a professional review.

4. Action Planning for Future Growth: Based on the insights gained, learn how to set actionable goals for personal development that align with your long-term relationship and career aspirations.

By systematically applying these professional techniques to your personal life, you enhance your emotional intelligence and improve your capacity to handle future personal and professional relationships with greater awareness and effectiveness. Chapter 2 will equip you with the tools to reflect on past experiences in a structured manner, ensuring that you continue to grow and learn from each life chapter.

Reflect on the transformative journey your Closure Performance Review has initiated:

- How has my perspective on the person or situation changed after this introspective review?

- What steps will I take to safeguard myself from future resentment?

- How does embracing forgiveness enhance my quality of life and relationships?

- How will I apply the lessons from this review to enrich my interactions, both personally and professionally?

The Closure Performance Review is a continuous practice fostering self-awareness, healing, and growth, laying the groundwork for a life enriched with understanding, forgiveness, and open-hearted connections. By embracing this process, you empower yourself to break free from the chains of resentment, paving the way for genuine healing and cultivating healthier relationships in the future. Each step taken in this journey brings you closer to a place of inner peace, where past wounds no longer define you, and the light of hope guides you toward a brighter tomorrow.

As you move forward with this newfound perspective, Chapter 2, "Reflecting and Learning: The Exit Interview Protocol," builds upon these foundational elements. In this next chapter, we delve deeper into the structured reflections used in professional exit interviews and adapt them to personal relationships. This approach provides a disciplined framework for introspection, allowing you to systematically unpack the dynamics of past interactions and understand their emotional underpinnings. Through guided questions and structured feedback, you will learn to articulate your needs and desires more clearly, setting the stage for future relationships that are both fulfilling and resilient. This systematic review not only aids in emotional liberation but also equips you with the tools to apply these insights, ensuring ongoing personal growth and a healthier emotional landscape as you step into the next chapter of your life.

2

REFLECTING AND LEARNING - THE EXIT INTERVIEW PROTOCOL

This chapter introduces the concept of the "Exit Interview Protocol," a structured approach that adapts professional exit interview techniques to personal relationship endings. This method guides readers through detailed introspection and evaluation, mirroring the closure process often used in professional environments to enhance understanding and growth after a personal relationship concludes. By applying these structured techniques, individuals can systematically dissect the components of their past relationships, identifying key lessons and areas for personal development.

This approach helps to process emotions and achieve closure. It transforms this understanding into actionable insights, much like a professional performance review aims to convert feedback into career advancement opportunities. By drawing parallels between the exit strategies used in professional settings and those that can be applied to personal scenarios, the Exit Interview Protocol offers a unique lens through which individuals can view their interpersonal relationships.

The chapter will delve into the practical application of this protocol, breaking down each step to ensure that readers can engage deeply with the process. It will cover the preparation for the interview, including setting emotional objectives and creating an environment conducive to open and honest reflection. The chapter's core will guide readers through crafting and responding to specific, tailored questions that probe the dynamics of the relationship, the contributions of each party, and the reasons behind its dissolution.

To further enrich the protocol, the chapter will incorporate exercises designed to foster emotional intelligence and resilience, such as recognizing emotional triggers and learning to respond rather than react. This holistic approach not only ensures a thorough analysis of past relationships but also prepares individuals for future interpersonal successes, both personal and professional.

In summary, the Exit Interview Protocol bridges recognizing the past and preparing for the future, enabling readers to harness their experiences and turn them into a foundation for growth and self-improvement.

Understanding the Role of Closure in Personal Growth

Just as professional exit interviews empower individuals to resolve issues and pave the way for future improvements, a structured self-review of personal relationships can lead to profound emotional and psychological healing. This process involves examining the relationship's dynamics, identifying strengths and shortcomings, and understanding emotional triggers, which can foster more resilient future relationships. By recognizing and addressing these elements, individuals can move forward with greater self-awareness and emotional clarity, transforming past experiences into valuable learning opportunities.

- Exercise: Conduct Your Exit Interview

Reflect on a past relationship and answer the following questions to guide your introspection. Write down your responses to clarify your thoughts and feelings. This exercise is designed to help you dissect the complexity of your interactions and extract meaningful insights that can foster personal growth and healthier future relationships.

1. What were the positive aspects of this relationship?

Reflect on the strengths of the relationship. Consider communication, support, shared values, or fun times. Recognizing these can help you understand what to look for and cultivate in future relationships.

- Answer: _____

_____

_____

2. What were the challenges or issues I encountered?

Identify specific problems that arose, whether they were communication breakdowns, misaligned values, or other conflicts. Understanding these challenges helps pinpoint what may need to change in your relationship approach or what red flags to watch out for in the future.

- Answer: _____

_____

_____

3. What have I learned from this relationship that can help me in the future?

Extract critical lessons from the positives and the challenges. Consider how these insights influence your relationship choices, communication styles, and personal boundaries.

- Answer: _____

_____

_____

This structured self-review concerns closure, learning, and growing from past experiences. It encourages you to approach personal growth with the same seriousness and constructive mindset as a professional evaluation. This exercise can help you better understand your needs and desires by setting the stage for future success in personal and even professional relationships. It equips you to seek out and foster fulfilling and growth-oriented relationships, inspiring hope, and optimism for the future.

Broadened Strategies for Learning from Past Relationships

1. Objective Reflection: Review the relationship without emotional bias, aiming to understand rather than judge. This helps identify factual events and behaviors that led to the relationship's outcome. By focusing on facts rather than feelings, you can more accurately pinpoint what worked and what didn't, fostering a clearer perspective on personal tendencies and relational dynamics.

2. Feedback Analysis: Like receiving feedback in a professional review, assess the feedback (both spoken and unspoken) given throughout the self-awareness and igniting a proactive approach to personal growth. By methodically analyzing the relationship's dynamics, you can pave the way for future relationships that are healthier and more fulfilling, instilling a sense of hope and motivation for the journey ahead.

Extending the Exercise for Comprehensive Insights

1. How did my emotional responses influence the relationship's dynamic?

Consider moments when your emotional reactions might have escalated conflicts or, conversely, helped resolve them. Understanding your emotional influence can guide you in managing emotions more effectively in future interactions.

- Answer: _____

_____

2. What lessons can I take from this relationship? How did communication styles, expectations, and personal differences influence the relationship dynamics? This analysis helps you understand how your actions and reactions contributed to the relationship's health or issues, providing critical insights into your interpersonal communication skills.

- Answer: _____

_____

_____

3. Actionable Insights: Based on your reflections and analysis, develop actionable insights. Determine what changes or improvements can be made in your personal development and future relationships. This might involve improving communication skills, learning to set more explicit boundaries, or even recognizing and changing certain behaviors that may have negatively impacted your relationships.

4. Resilience Building: This reflective process builds emotional resilience. Understanding and accepting the end of a relationship can strengthen your emotional health and prepare you for future interpersonal interactions. Each reflection and adjustment contributes to a more resilient emotional state, allowing you to handle personal setbacks and conflicts with more remarkable composure and less distress.

5. Pattern Recognition: Identify recurring relationship patterns and consider their roots. Are there specific traits or behaviors that consistently contribute to conflict or dissatisfaction? Recognizing

these patterns can illuminate underlying issues, such as dependency traits, communication faults, or mismatched relationship expectations.

6. Preventative Strategies: Once patterns are recognized and insights are formed, develop preventative strategies to avoid repeating past mistakes. This might include establishing new communication guidelines for yourself, methods for handling conflict, or even criteria for choosing future partners more wisely.

7. Integration of Learnings: Integrate the lessons learned from past relationships into your everyday life. Apply these insights in romantic contexts, friendships, and professional relationships. This holistic application reinforces the learnings and helps cement them as part of your ongoing personal growth journey.

Expanding these strategies from Chapter 1's foundation, you can turn past relationship experiences into valuable lessons that enhance your personal life and interactions in all spheres. Each strategy builds upon the last, creating a comprehensive framework for continual improvement and a deeper understanding of oneself and others.

Enhanced Interactive Exercise: The Personal Exit Interview

Dedicate time for an in-depth session to apply the Exit Interview Protocol. Explore the intricacies of the relationship using structured feedback and reflective questions to gain a comprehensive understanding of its impact on your personal growth:

1. What patterns in my or my partner's behavior have I noticed during this relationship?

Reflect on recurring behaviors or prominent reactions during the relationship. Identify constructive or destructive patterns, such as communication styles, conflict resolution tactics, or emotional responses, and consider how they shaped the relationship dynamics.

- Answer: _____

_____

_____

2. How have these patterns affected the relationship's outcome?

Analyze how identified patterns contributed to the relationship's success or difficulties. Did they foster understanding and intimacy or lead to misunderstandings and conflicts? This reflection helps pinpoint specific areas that either need reinforcement or change.

- Answer: _____

_____

_____

3. What personal strengths have supported me through the relationship, and what areas do I need to develop further?

Recognize the strengths that helped maintain the relationship, such as empathy, patience, or honesty. Simultaneously, identify areas for development like assertiveness, listening skills, or openness to compromise, which could improve future relationship dynamics.

- Answer: _____

_____

_____

This exercise, a powerful tool for fostering deeper relationships, ended?

Reflect on the end phase of the relationship to extract lessons about closure, communication during stressful times, and personal limits. This can provide valuable insights into handling ending scenarios more gracefully in the future.

- Answer: _____

_____

_____

4. How can I apply these insights to improve my overall interpersonal skills?

Use the gleaned insights to develop strategies for enhancing interpersonal skills across all types of relationships, not just romantic ones. This might involve practicing better communication, increasing emotional intelligence, or learning to set and respect boundaries more effectively.

- Answer: _____

_____

_____

This expanded approach enhances personal understanding and growth following a relationship's end. It equips you with practical skills and strategies to improve your future personal and professional relationships. The exercise emphasizes a holistic reflection process where each insight contributes to a broader application, encouraging ongoing development and improvement in all areas of life.

Real-Life Scenario and Author Insights

- Real-World Scenario: IT consultant Michael utilized the Exit Interview Protocol after a significant relationship ended. He identified communication breakdowns and mismatched life goals as critical issues. Michael improved his communication skills by applying structured reflection techniques and gained insights into aligning personal and professional goals. This comprehensive approach helped him better manage expectations in his personal life and adapt his professional interactions to be more effective and collaborative. His ability to articulate and negotiate his needs improved dramatically, leading to healthier personal relationships and more successful team projects.

- Author Insights: Nakisha Gregory notes, "Understanding the closure of personal relationships through a structured review can illuminate underlying patterns that affect personal and professional relationships." Jahnni Allen adds, "This methodical approach allows individuals to close chapters in their lives with clarity and peace, setting the foundation for future growth in all aspects of life." They both emphasize that the skills developed through such introspective practices are transferable and have profound impacts beyond personal healing. By critically assessing past interactions, individuals learn to communicate more effectively, set more explicit boundaries, and develop greater emotional intelligence, which is invaluable in both personal and professional environments.

Additional Reflections and Applications

- Further Insights: Michael's experience highlights the dual benefits of the Exit Interview Protocol. Not only does it facilitate personal understanding and emotional healing, but it also enhances professional capabilities. For instance, his improved communication skills led to more effective conflict resolution and better project management at his job, demonstrating how personal development directly contributes to professional efficacy.

- Broader Implications: This scenario underscores the interconnectedness of personal growth and professional success. As individuals refine their interpersonal skills and become more adept at managing personal relationships, they enhance their professional interactions concurrently. This symbiosis is particularly relevant in professions requiring teamwork, leadership, and negotiation skills.

- Encouragement for continuous improvement: Nakisha and Jahnni encourage readers to view each personal or professional relationship as an opportunity for continuous learning and improvement. By regularly engaging in reflective practices like the Exit Interview Protocol, individuals can maintain a cycle of growth and development that perpetuates success across all areas of their lives.

Through these insights and real-world applications, the chapter aims to inspire readers to embrace structured reflection as a tool for navigating the end of relationships and as a lifelong personal and professional development strategy. This holistic approach ensures that individuals are constantly evolving and adapting, ready to meet the challenges and opportunities that lie ahead.

Conclusion and Transition to Next Steps

As you complete your Exit Interview, reflect on the emotional liberation and personal insights gained. This chapter sets the stage for applying these learnings to future personal relationships and professional interactions, reinforcing the interconnected growth in both domains. By thoroughly understanding the dynamics of past relationships and your role within them, you can better navigate future interactions with a clearer perspective and enhanced emotional intelligence.

In the next chapter, "Evolving Through Introspection: Charting Personal Growth," we will explore how to turn the Exit Interview's insights into actionable strategies for future relationships, ensuring continuous personal development and emotional well-being. This chapter will delve deeper into the mechanisms of introspection, teaching you to systematically examine your thoughts, feelings, and behaviors to foster ongoing growth.

Key Focus Areas of Chapter 3:

1. Deepening Self-Awareness: Learn advanced techniques for introspection beyond initial reflections, focusing on understanding deep-seated beliefs and biases that influence your behaviors and relationships.

2. Developing Emotional Agility: Based on the insights gained, explore how to manage and adapt your emotional responses. This includes cultivating resilience and flexibility in handling interpersonal challenges and stress.

3. Setting Personal Growth Goals: Based on your introspective findings, establish clear, measurable goals. This section will guide you in setting realistic expectations for yourself and your personal and professional relationships.

4. Implementing Reflective Practices: Introduce regular reflective practices into your daily routine to keep your growth on track. Techniques such as journaling, meditation, and mindfulness exercises will be discussed to help maintain a continuous loop of introspection and improvement.

5. Applying Insights to Relationship Building: Use your self-discoveries to enhance how you form and maintain relationships. This will cover communication strategies, boundary setting, and fostering mutually supportive relationships that promote personal and collective growth.

6. Integrating Professional Development: Translate personal insights into your professional life to improve leadership, teamwork, and communication skills. Understand how personal growth directly impacts professional effectiveness and career progression.

Conclusion and Action Plan: The chapter concludes with a practical action plan for integrating these reflective practices into your everyday life, ensuring that personal growth becomes a consistent part of your journey toward a fulfilling and balanced life.

Building on the foundations set in previous chapters, Chapter 3 will equip you with the tools to reflect upon and understand past experiences and actively shape your future, creating a life rich in growth, learning, and meaningful connections.

3

EVOLVING THROUGH INTROSPECTION: CHARTING PERSONAL GROWTH

Building from the reflective insights developed in Chapter 2, "Evolving Through Introspection: Charting Personal Growth," delves deeper into applying reflective practices to foster continuous personal and professional development. This chapter underscores the critical role of self-awareness and emotional agility in nurturing personal growth, aiming to convert the introspective insights from the Exit Interview Protocol into actionable strategies for future relationships and ongoing self-improvement. It emphasizes the transformation of these insights into a structured framework that supports cultivating a balanced, resilient self. Through detailed guidance, this chapter aids in the practical application of understanding personal emotional landscapes, enabling the reader to navigate complex interpersonal dynamics with greater ease and confidence.

Additionally, this chapter introduces various techniques for embedding these insights into daily life, ensuring that personal development is about introspection and active and conscious application. It covers methods for turning self-awareness into self-regulation and emotional agility into effective communication and leadership skills. Integrating these practices aims to equip individuals with the tools needed to transform challenges into opportunities for growth, improving both personal well-being and professional efficacy.

Readers will learn to establish a continuous loop of feedback and refinement in their behavior, encouraging lifelong learning and self-discovery. This structured approach to personal development is designed to foster immediate improvements in handling personal and professional relationships and long-term resilience and adaptability, preparing individuals for future challenges and opportunities.

Deepening Self-Awareness

This section focuses on enhancing your understanding of your emotional patterns and triggers. Techniques such as deep reflective journaling, personality tests, and mindfulness practices are introduced to help you explore underlying motivations and the root causes of your behaviors. This deeper level of self-awareness is essential for recognizing habitual reactions that may have hindered past relationships or limited personal growth. By becoming more aware of these patterns, you can make conscious choices that lead to more positive outcomes in personal and professional interactions.

- Exercise: Deep Reflective Journaling

Dedicate time each day to write about your reactions to daily interactions. Note any patterns or consistent themes that arise. This practice will help you become more mindful of your habitual responses and more adept at managing them proactively. Questions to guide your journaling might include:

- What emotions did I feel today and why?

- How did I handle difficult moments, and what could I improve?

- What brought me joy, and how can I incorporate more of that into my life?

This exercise not only aids in recognizing and understanding emotional responses but also helps track your progress over time. What triggered a strong reaction one month may have less effect as you develop greater emotional control and understanding.

Developing Emotional Agility

Based on your reflective findings, learn to manage, and adapt your emotional responses more effectively. This section teaches techniques for emotional regulation, such as cognitive reframing and stress management strategies, which are vital for transforming insights into emotional resilience. This agility lets you handle personal and professional challenges with excellent composure and insight.

- Technique: Cognitive Reframing

- Learn to identify and alter negative thought patterns that may cause emotional distress or reactive behaviors. Reframing these thoughts can change your emotional response to various situations, leading to more positive outcomes. For example, if you feel upset about a work situation, try reframing it as an opportunity to learn something new or improve a particular skill.

- Stress Management Strategies

- Incorporate stress management techniques such as progressive muscle relaxation, guided visualization, or breathing exercises into your routine. These practices help reduce stress in the moment and build long-term resilience by enhancing your capacity to deal with stressors effectively.

You are better equipped to face challenges and transform potential conflicts into personal growth and professional development opportunities by developing emotional agility. These skills are crucial for anyone looking to lead a balanced and fulfilling life, as they enhance your ability to navigate the complexities of modern relationships and professional environments with grace and effectiveness.

Technique: Cognitive Reframing

Learn to identify and adjust negative thought patterns. Practice turning a common negative thought into a positive or neutral statement and observe how it changes your emotional response. This technique empowers you to control your outlook on daily challenges, enhancing resilience and promoting a more positive mental state. For example, instead of thinking, "I never do anything right," reframe it to "I make mistakes like everyone else, but I always learn from them."

Setting Personal Growth Goals

Based on your introspective insights, this part guides you in setting specific, measurable, and achievable personal growth goals. These goals are tailored to strengthen areas of weakness identified during your introspection and capitalize on your strengths. It emphasizes the importance of aligning these goals with your values and long-term objectives, both personally and professionally.

- Goal-Setting Workshop:

- Host a session to define your goals using the SMART criteria (Specific, Measurable, Achievable, Relevant, Time-bound). Examples include improving communication skills, managing stress, or developing new relationships supporting your growth. This workshop can be a dynamic session where you brainstorm potential goals, evaluate them based on the SMART criteria, and refine them to ensure they align with your overall life objectives.

Implementing Reflective Practices

Encourage the integration of regular reflective practices into your daily life. These can include meditation, mindfulness, and continued journaling. This section provides a structured plan for making these practices part of your routine, ensuring they become habits that support ongoing growth.

- Daily Mindfulness Routine:

- Introduce a simple mindfulness routine to be practiced each morning or evening, focusing on breathing techniques and body scans to enhance present-moment awareness. This routine could start with five minutes of focused breathing followed by a brief body scan to identify and release any physical tension. As the practice becomes a habit, you can gradually extend the time and incorporate more mindfulness exercises that foster deeper awareness and calm.

Each component—cognitive reframing, goal-setting, and reflective practices—plays a vital role in developing a comprehensive personal development plan. Together, they help you cope with immediate challenges and lay a strong foundation for long-term growth and fulfillment. By routinely applying these practices, you ensure that personal development is an active and ongoing process, constantly refined as you gain new insights and achieve new milestones in your personal and professional life.

Applying Insights to Relationship Building:

Utilize the power of deepened self-awareness and emotional agility to enhance your relationship-building skills. This guide offers practical advice on effective communication, empathetic listening, and setting healthy boundaries. These strategies are crucial for fostering supportive and enriching relationships and are easily applicable in both personal and professional settings. You can transform your interactions by honing your interpersonal skills, leading to more productive and satisfying engagements.

Scenario:

- Emily and the Project Team Conflict: a project manager, Emily was consistently frustrated with her team's lack of engagement during meetings. After applying the introspective insights gained from her Exit Interview Protocol, Emily recognized her communication style was often more directive than inclusive. She used her new empathetic listening skills and asked open-ended questions to encourage dialogue. Over the next few meetings, she noticed a significant improvement in team interaction, with members expressing more ideas and showing increased commitment to project goals.

- Insight from Authors and Specialists:

- Nakisha Gregory: "Understanding your communication style and how it affects others can lead to professional and personal breakthroughs in relationship management. Emily's shift from directive to inclusive communication exemplifies how subtle changes can profoundly affect team dynamics."

- Jahnni Allen: "Setting boundaries is also essential for healthy relationships. It's about respecting your limits and expressing them clearly, which Emily demonstrated by managing her expectations of her team and adjusting her leadership style to suit their needs better."

Specialist Insight—Dr. Alex Rendon, Communication Psychologist: "Empathetic listening is not just hearing words; it's about truly understanding the emotions and intentions behind them. When leaders like Emily implement this in a team setting, it fosters an environment of trust and openness, which is crucial for collaborative success."

This chapter will explore various techniques and exercises individuals can practice enhancing their communication skills, such as role-playing scenarios focusing on active listening and nonverbal communication cues. It would also provide guidelines on articulating and negotiating personal boundaries effectively, ensuring that relationships are respectful and mutually beneficial. These practices, rooted in self-awareness and emotional agility, equip individuals with the tools to build and maintain healthy, supportive relationships across all areas of life.

- Interactive Workshop: Effective Communication

-   Conduct role-play exercises to practice assertive communication and empathetic listening, enhancing your ability to engage constructively in personal and professional relationships.

Integrating Professional Development

Translate personal growth into professional advancement by applying your emotional and interpersonal insights to your work environment. This includes enhancing leadership skills, improving teamwork, and managing work relationships.

Professional Growth Plan:

Create a plan that outlines steps to take your insights into the workplace, such as seeking feedback from peers, undertaking leadership training, or engaging in team-building activities. This proactive approach enhances your professional skills and improves your interpersonal relationships at work. Tailor this plan to your specific career goals and personal insights, ensuring that it reflects both your strengths and areas for improvement.

- Implementation Examples:

Seeking Feedback: Schedule feedback sessions regularly with peers and supervisors to gain a clearer understanding of how your behavior impacts others and where you can improve.

- Leadership Training: Enroll in workshops or seminars focusing on developing leadership qualities congruent with your personal growth goals, such as effective communication, conflict resolution, and team motivation.

- Team-Building Activities: Organize or participate in team-building exercises to help mend or strengthen relationships and improve team cohesion and overall morale.

Conclusion and Action Plan:

The chapter concludes with a comprehensive action plan to apply the reflective practices consistently and effectively, ensuring they contribute to a holistic approach to personal development. This plan will guide you through setting regular check-ins with yourself, adjusting goals as needed, and continually seeking new ways to apply your insights. This dynamic approach to personal development ensures that your growth is sustained and responsive to your changing needs and circumstances.

- Regular Check-ins: Establish a routine, such as bi-weekly or monthly reviews, where you assess your progress towards your personal and professional goals and make necessary adjustments.

- Goal Adjustment: Modify your goals flexibly based on the feedback you receive and the insights you gain through ongoing reflection and practice.

- Continuous Application: Seek new opportunities to apply your insights in different contexts, expanding your ability to handle diverse situations with resilience and understanding.

By the end of Chapter 3, you will have a robust framework for using introspection to understand past experiences and proactively shape your future, fostering a life characterized by growth, learning, and meaningful connections in all realms.

As you move into Chapter 4, "Embracing Growth: Cultivating Resilience and Authenticity," the focus shifts from introspection to active cultivation of resilience and authenticity in all aspects of life. This next chapter will explore strategies to enhance your ability to bounce back from challenges and to live authentically in alignment with your values and insights. Through practical exercises and real-world applications, Chapter 4 will provide you with the tools to withstand adversities and thrive amidst them, reinforcing the foundational work done in the previous chapters and pushing further into developing a resilient and authentic self.

4

EMBRACING GROWTH: CULTIVATING RESILIENCE AND AUTHENTICITY

Building on the reflective practices from Chapter 3, "Embracing Growth: Cultivating Resilience and Authenticity," explores how to actively foster resilience and live authentically, aligning daily actions with personal values and insights. This chapter focuses on strengthening the ability to recover from setbacks and maintain integrity in both personal and professional realms, ensuring that growth is not only about adapting to change but also about thriving amidst it. It delves into practical methods for developing resilience through mindset shifts and behavior adjustments that facilitate rapid recovery and sustained progress. The chapter introduces various dynamic resilience-building techniques, such as emotional conditioning, strategic optimism, and adaptive flexibility, which empower individuals to transform challenges into stepping stones for personal development and success. These techniques are designed to help individuals withstand adversity and emerge more robust and resourceful, turning potential obstacles into opportunities for personal triumph and professional advancement.

Furthermore, this chapter emphasizes the integration of authenticity into everyday life, advocating for a lifestyle that reflects one's true self across all situations. It explores how authentic living enhances decision-making and fosters more profound connections with others by staying true to one's principles and values. To support this, the chapter offers exercises in moral alignment, where readers assess their daily choices against their core beliefs, ensuring consistency and integrity in their actions. These exercises encourage self-reflection and mindfulness, which are crucial for anyone seeking to live authentically and influence others positively. By consistently aligning daily actions with deeply held values, individuals can lead more coherent and satisfying lives that resonate with those around them, strengthening relationships and building trust.

Additionally, practical examples illustrate how these resilience and authenticity strategies can be applied in personal and professional crises. By weaving in stories of individuals who have exemplified resilience and authenticity in various contexts, the chapter motivates and provides a clear roadmap for readers to apply these concepts in their lives. This holistic approach helps to cultivate a resilient mindset that is not just reactive to adversity but proactive in embracing life's complexities, ensuring continuous growth and a fulfilling life trajectory. Stories such as a business leader navigating company crises with transparency and a healthcare professional maintaining compassionate care under stress exemplify how these principles can be effectively implemented. These narratives serve as inspiration and practical guides demonstrating the transformative power of resilience and authenticity in overcoming challenges and achieving meaningful success.

Enhancing Coping Strategies

The chapter introduces robust coping strategies that equip you to handle life's challenges more effectively. Techniques such as adaptive problem-solving, which involves viewing challenges from multiple perspectives and brainstorming various solutions, are crucial in building resilience. Additionally, stress inoculation training, which prepares individuals to handle stress before it becomes overwhelming, is explored to help you manage and anticipate stressors proactively. Building on the insights from Chapter 3, where individuals learn to recognize and adjust negative thought patterns, these coping strategies provide practical tools to navigate difficult situations with resilience and authenticity. Individuals can proactively address challenges by incorporating adaptive problem-solving techniques and stress management strategies into daily routines while maintaining emotional balance and clarity. This proactive approach aligns with the concept of emotional agility introduced in the previous chapter, where individuals learn to manage and adapt their emotional responses effectively, enhancing their ability to cope with stressors and setbacks.

Authenticity in Action

Living authentically is emphasized as a continuous practice of making choices congruent with one's true self. This section provides strategies for regular self-reflection to ensure one's actions consistently reflect one's values. It also discusses the importance of vulnerability in authenticity, encouraging openness about one's feelings and uncertainties, which can lead to deeper connections and a stronger sense of self-worth. Building on the theme of authenticity explored in Chapter 3, where individuals learned to align their actions with their core values, this section encourages readers to cultivate authenticity through intentional decision-making and vulnerability. By practicing authentic decision-making exercises and embracing vulnerability, individuals can strengthen their sense of self and deepen their connections with others. This aligns with the concept of living authentically introduced in the previous chapter, where individuals learned to integrate authenticity into their daily lives, enhancing personal satisfaction and fostering more profound connections with others.

- Exercise: Authentic Decision Making

- Practice exercises that involve making small, everyday decisions based on your core values. Reflect on these decisions through journaling or discussions to evaluate how well they align with your true self, enhancing your ability to act authentically under pressure. By incorporating authentic decision-making exercises into daily routines, individuals can better understand their values and strengthen their ability to act authentically in various situations. This exercise builds on the principles of authenticity introduced in the previous chapter, providing practical tools to align actions with values and enhance personal integrity.

Resilience Through Relationships

This chapter covers how to utilize personal and professional relationships to enhance resilience. It underscores the importance of social support systems and how they can provide emotional sustenance and practical assistance during challenging times.

Techniques for nurturing these relationships, such as regular communication, mutual support activities, and collaborative problem-solving, are discussed to emphasize their role in resilience-building. It delves into the dynamics of building solid and supportive networks that offer comfort during crises and promote ongoing mutual growth and empowerment.

In addition, this section highlights the value of diverse relationships in broadening perspectives and strengthening personal resilience. Engaging with various individuals can give different viewpoints and strategies for coping with and overcoming adversity. The chapter also addresses the importance of being supportive in others' lives, which can enhance your resilience by fostering a sense of purpose and community.

- Practical Exercise: Building Your Support Network

 - Engage in activities designed to map out and strengthen your current network. Identify key individuals who provide emotional, informational, or instrumental support. Plan and initiate activities to deepen these connections, such as regular meetups, joint projects, or support groups.

- Insight from Relationship Experts:

 - Dr. Maria Gonzalez, a social psychologist, explains, "Resilience is often seen as a personal quality, but it's deeply rooted in our interactions and relationships. Our networks can act as mirrors reflecting our strengths and areas for growth, which is invaluable for personal development."

- Real-World Example:

- Carlos's Community Initiative: After recovering from a personal loss, Carlos started a community group focused on mental health awareness. This initiative helped him find a supportive community and empowered others to build resilience through shared experiences and resources. His story illustrates how taking active steps to create and participate in supportive communities can bolster personal and collective resilience.

By integrating these insights and practices, readers can develop a more resilient approach to relationships that not only help them withstand life's challenges but also enriches their personal and professional lives. This chapter encourages active participation in and cultivation of relationships that are not only supportive but also reciprocal, enhancing the resilience of the entire community.

- Technique: Resilience Training

- Engage in resilience training exercises focusing on developing a positive mindset, such as gratitude journaling and scenario planning to anticipate and prepare for potential challenges. This proactive approach helps mitigate the impact of stress and fosters a resilient mindset.

Living Authentically

Authenticity involves understanding and staying true to your values and beliefs. This section guides aligning your actions with your core values, enhancing personal satisfaction and integrity in your interactions.

- Insight from Authors and Specialists:

- Nakisha Gregory: "Living authentically isn't just about being true to yourself; crafting a life that consistently reflects your values, even under pressure. Authenticity fortifies relationships and builds trust in professional settings."

- Jahnni Allen: "Authenticity in the workplace leads to better decision-making and leadership. When you're true to your values, your choices align with your organization's goals, leading to greater effectiveness and fulfillment. These practices also translate into your personal life."

- Exercise: Values Clarification Workshop

- Conduct a workshop to help clarify and articulate your core values. This exercise involves listing your values, ranking them in order of importance, and identifying ways to integrate them into your daily life and work.

Applying Insights to Relationship Building

This section expands on the insights gained in previous chapters to improve relationships further. It emphasizes advanced communication strategies, more profound empathetic listening, and the assertive expression of needs and boundaries, which are crucial for developing robust personal and professional relationships.

- Real-World Scenario:

- Tom and Interdepartmental Collaboration: Tom struggled with cross-departmental communication as an operations manager. Applying his insights into empathetic listening and authentic communication improved collaboration between his team and the IT department, leading to more efficient project outcomes and reduced conflicts.

Integrating Professional Development

Continue translating personal growth into professional advancement by applying emotional and interpersonal insights to enhance leadership and teamwork. This section focuses on practical applications in the workplace, such as leading with empathy, managing diversity, and fostering an inclusive work environment.

- Professional Growth Plan Update:

- Update your professional growth plan to include new insights and strategies learned about resilience and authenticity. This might involve seeking roles challenging your leadership abilities or starting a mentorship program to develop and share resilience strategies with colleagues.

Conclusion and Future Directions

"Embracing Growth: Cultivating Resilience and Authenticity" concludes by underlining the empowering nature of ongoing personal development and the continuous application of the insights gained throughout this journey. It advocates for a lifelong commitment to learning, growing, and adapting, ensuring you remain resilient and authentic, no matter the challenges ahead. This commitment is not merely a strategy for managing difficulties but a proactive approach to cultivating a fulfilling, purpose-driven life, empowering you to take control of your personal and professional development.

- Final Reflection:

- Reflect on how the journey through these chapters has equipped you with tools to cope with and thrive amidst life's complexities. Encourage ongoing engagement with these practices, emphasizing that actual growth is a perpetual process of adaptation and learning. Consider the transformations you have already observed in yourself and envision how these can continue to evolve. Let this reflection serve as a motivational close that empowers you to embrace your growth journey enthusiastically and confidently.

- Looking Ahead:

- As you move forward, consider how the principles of resilience and authenticity can be further integrated into your daily life and professional endeavors. Regularly revisit your goals and strategies, adapting them as your circumstances and insights evolve. Expand your support networks and seek personal and professional development opportunities through workshops, courses, and community involvement. This proactive engagement will enrich your understanding and application of these core concepts.

This chapter serves as a bridge to future growth opportunities. It prepares you for a lifelong personal and professional development journey rooted in resilience and authenticity. It sets the stage for deeper exploration into personal growth areas such as emotional intelligence, leadership, and social responsibility. By adopting a mindset that views every experience as an opportunity for growth, you are better prepared to meet future challenges and harness potential setbacks as catalysts for development.

- Call to Action:

  - The chapter concludes with a call to action, urging readers to take proactive steps toward their development by engaging in new experiences that challenge their comfort zones, actively seeking feedback, and continually applying the concepts of resilience and authenticity to various aspects of their lives. It also encourages readers to share their stories of growth and resilience with others, fostering a community of continuous learning and mutual support.

As we transition to the next chapter, "Reclaiming Your Narrative: Crafting Your Story," the focus will shift from internal growth to how you can articulate and share your journey with the world. This next chapter will explore how to craft your narrative to reflect your journey of resilience and authenticity and inspire and influence others. Reclaiming your narrative, you'll learn to communicate your story effectively, making it a powerful tool for personal expression and professional engagement. This narrative process will help solidify your growth and allow you to contribute meaningfully to personal and professional development dialogues.

5

RECLAIMING YOUR NARRATIVE: CRAFTING YOUR STORY

After exploring the intricate balance between personal and professional growth through the themes of resilience and authenticity in "Love Layoff," Chapter 5, "Reclaiming Your Narrative: Crafting Your Story," shifts focus to how individuals can articulate and redefine their personal and professional journeys. This chapter provides a structured approach to reclaiming your narrative, integrating the wisdom gained from love and labor experiences to guide you toward a future brimming with opportunity and personal fulfillment. It emphasizes the transformative power of storytelling in shaping perceptions, influencing relationships, and steering professional careers. By harnessing the lessons from both successful and challenging experiences, readers are encouraged to construct a narrative that not only reflects their past but also actively shapes their future.

This chapter also delves into the psychological and emotional benefits of effective storytelling, explaining how a well-crafted narrative can enhance self-understanding, build confidence, and open doors to new opportunities. Through practical exercises and insightful examples, readers will learn how to weave their varied experiences into a cohesive story that highlights their resilience, adaptability, and authenticity. The chapter aims to empower readers to take ownership of their stories, ensuring they resonate with integrity and purpose across all aspects of their lives, from personal interactions to professional engagements. This holistic approach to narrative crafting helps individuals not just recount their past, but reclaim control of their life's direction, embodying the lessons learned to foster ongoing growth and success.

This transformative process involves deeply exploring past experiences, recognizing their impact on your current identity, and utilizing these insights to mold a compelling future narrative. The chapter emphasizes the importance of storytelling as a powerful tool for self-expression and connection, influencing personal relationships and professional interactions. It highlights how effectively crafted stories can bridge the gap between individual identity and broader societal contexts, enabling a more profound engagement with diverse audiences. By reflecting on significant life events and articulating the lessons learned, individuals can develop narratives that resonate on multiple levels, providing clarity and motivation not only to themselves but also inspiring others.

Additionally, the chapter discusses the strategic use of narrative to enhance personal branding, outlining how to align personal stories with professional goals to create impactful career narratives. Through step-by-step guidelines, readers learn how to polish and present their stories in ways that highlight their unique strengths and visions, making them memorable and influential in both networking settings and formal presentations. The chapter also introduces techniques for integrating emotional intelligence and cultural sensitivity into storytelling, ensuring that narratives are not only authentic but also respectful and inclusive, thereby fostering stronger connections and collaborations in increasingly diverse environments.

Insights from Authors:

- Nakisha Gregory comments on the power of narrative, "Stories are the core of how we understand ourselves and the world. Reclaiming your narrative means taking control of that story and making it work for you, not just in healing from past wounds but also in forging your path forward."

- Jahnni Allen provides a perspective on the intersection of personal and professional growth, "The skills you develop in overcoming personal challenges are invaluable in the workplace. Your story of resilience becomes a testament to your ability to adapt and thrive in changing environments."

Professional Insights:

- Dr. Helen Fisher, a renowned psychologist, stresses the therapeutic aspects of storytelling, "Crafting your narrative can be a form of cognitive restructuring, helping to reframe and reinterpret your past experiences in a way that highlights your strengths and resilience."

- Markus Weber, a career coach, advises on professional storytelling, "In the professional realm, your story is your brand. It communicates who you are, what you stand for, and where you aim to go. A well-crafted narrative can distinguish you in a competitive job market."

Practical Applications:

The chapter guides readers through several practical exercises designed to help them craft and refine their narratives:

1. Timeline Creation - Build a visual timeline of significant life events, both personal and professional, to identify patterns, pivotal moments, and turning points.

2. Theme Identification - Analyze your timeline to identify recurring themes or lessons that have shaped your growth. This could include themes of resilience, transformation, or discovery.

3. Narrative Workshops—Participate in or organize workshops focused on narrative development, where participants can share their stories in a supportive environment and gain insights and feedback.

4. Digital Storytelling—Use multimedia tools to create digital stories that can be shared on social media or professional platforms, enhancing your online presence and connecting with broader audiences.

Case Studies:

- Case Study of Julia: A professional who transitioned from a corporate role to starting her own business after a significant layoff. Her story highlights how she used her layoff as a springboard to embrace her entrepreneurial spirit and redefine her career trajectory. Julia's narrative illustrates the power of resilience and proactive adaptation; she identified her core competencies and passion for design and transformed these into a successful interior design business. Her journey showcases how personal challenges can catalyze self-discovery and lead to new professional paths that align more closely with one's values and aspirations.

- Case Study of Tom: After a challenging breakup, Tom used his experiences to fuel his passion for mental health advocacy, reshaping his adversities into a professional mission supporting others. Tom's story demonstrates the therapeutic power of turning personal pain into a communal gain. By channeling his struggle into advocacy, Tom founded a nonprofit organization focused on mental health awareness and support for young adults, using his story to connect with and inspire others who are facing similar challenges.

By the end of Chapter 5, readers will have learned to articulate their personal and professional experiences compellingly and understand how to use their narratives as strategic tools for growth and connection. The chapter concludes with a call to action for readers to continuously evolve their stories as they encounter new experiences and insights, ensuring their narratives remain dynamic and reflect their authentic selves. This ongoing process of narrative development not only enhances personal identity and agency but also fosters deeper connections with others, making storytelling a pivotal element of both personal resilience and professional success.

6

CLARIFYING DEAL BREAKERS: ESTABLISHING NON-NEGOTIABLE POLICIES

As you've journeyed through the intricacies of navigating personal and professional growth, it's become evident that the boundaries we set in love and labor are crucial to our well-being. It's time to clarify your deal breakers and establish non-negotiable policies that honor your professional aspirations and personal fulfillment. Building upon the insights gained from previous chapters and the experiences of individuals like Candace, we'll construct a roadmap for setting boundaries that empower you to thrive in both spheres of life.

Outline: Clarifying Deal Breakers - Establishing Non-Negotiable Policies

1. Reflect on Your Experience

- Identify Priorities: Take a moment to reflect on the lessons learned from your past relationships or career endeavors. Consider what aspects were vital for your happiness and success. Let's follow Candace's journey. Like Alex, she faced a significant setback in her love life and realized the importance of prioritizing her needs and goals.

Acknowledge Patterns: Recognize recurring patterns or warning signs that have emerged in previous relationships or workplaces. Understanding these patterns can help you identify your non-negotiables more effectively. Candace acknowledged patterns of sacrificing her own well-being in relationships and made a commitment to prioritize self-care moving forward.

2. Define Your Boundaries

- Professional Boundaries: Clearly define your boundaries in the workplace, including expectations around workload, work-life balance, and treatment by colleagues or superiors. Establishing these boundaries is crucial for maintaining your well-being and productivity. Candace set boundaries around working hours and communication to ensure a healthy work-life balance.

- Personal Boundaries: Define your boundaries in relationships, covering communication, respect, and emotional support. Communicate these boundaries clearly to your partner to foster mutual understanding and respect. Candace established boundaries around respect for her time and emotions, refusing to tolerate dismissive behavior or emotional manipulation.

3. Communicate Your Deal Breakers

- Direct Communication: Communicate your deal breakers directly and assertively, whether in a professional setting or a personal relationship. Clearly express your needs and boundaries to ensure they are understood and respected. Candace had open and honest conversations with her employer and partner, clearly stating her non-negotiables and expectations.

- Consistent Enforcement: Consistently enforce your boundaries and deal breakers, addressing any violations promptly and assertively. Consistency is critical to maintaining respect for your boundaries over time. Candace remained firm in upholding her boundaries, addressing any breaches assertively and without compromise.

4. Align Your Policies with Your Values

- Professional Values: Ensure your non-negotiable policies align with your professional values and goals. Your boundaries should reflect what you stand for in your career and the standards you uphold. Candace's boundaries in the workplace were rooted in her values of integrity, respect, and work-life balance.

- Personal Values: Similarly, align your boundaries with your core values and beliefs. Your deal breakers should honor your individuality and protect your emotional well-being. Candace's boundaries were guided by her values of self-respect, honesty, and emotional authenticity.

5. Evaluate and Adjust as Needed

- Regular Assessment: Regularly assess your boundaries and deal breakers to ensure they continue to serve your needs effectively. Be open to adjusting them as your circumstances change or as you gain new insights. Candace periodically reviewed her boundaries, adjusting as needed to align with her evolving needs and goals.

- Flexibility: While upholding your non-negotiables is essential, allow yourself flexibility to adapt to changing situations or dynamics. Flexibility can help you navigate unforeseen challenges while staying true to your core values. Candace remained flexible in her approach to boundaries, recognizing the need to adapt to different contexts while staying true to her principles.

6. Seek Support and Accountability

- Professional Support: Seek support from mentors, colleagues, or professional networks to reinforce your boundaries and deal breakers in the workplace. Surround yourself with individuals who respect and uphold similar standards. Candace leaned on her professional network for support and guidance in maintaining her boundaries at work.

- Personal Support: Similarly, seek support from friends, family, or a therapist to uphold your relationship boundaries. A robust support system can provide validation and encouragement as you navigate challenging situations. Candace relied on her close friends and therapist to enforce her boundaries with her partner.

7. Embrace Self-Care and Reflection

- Self-Care Practices: Prioritize self-care practices that nurture your physical, emotional, and mental well-being. Self-care is essential for replenishing your energy and resilience as you navigate boundary-setting in both professional and personal contexts. Candace prioritized self-care activities such as meditation, exercise, and journaling to stay grounded and resilient.

- Reflection: Set aside time for reflection to assess how well your boundaries serve you and identify areas for improvement.

Regular reflection can deepen your self-awareness and empower you to make informed decisions about your boundaries. Candace regularly reflected on her boundary-setting journey, celebrating successes and learning from challenges.

8. Stay Committed to Growth

- Continuous Learning: Approach boundary-setting as a continuous learning and growth journey. Stay open to new insights and strategies that can enhance your boundary-setting skills over time. Candace remained committed to learning and growing in her ability to set and maintain healthy boundaries in both her professional and personal life.

- Resilience: Cultivate resilience to navigate setbacks or challenges that may arise as you enforce your boundaries. Resilience will empower you to stay true to your values and bounce back from adversity with strength and grace. Candace embraced resilience as she faced resistance or pushback while upholding her boundaries, staying steadfast in her commitment to self-respect and well-being.

9. Celebrate Your Progress

- Milestones: Celebrate milestones and achievements in your boundary-setting journey, no matter how small. Acknowledge your progress and growth as you honor your values and protect your well-being. Candace celebrated each milestone in her boundary-setting journey, recognizing the courage and resilience it took to assert her needs and priorities.

- Self-Appreciation: Practice self-appreciation and self-compassion as you navigate the challenges of setting and enforcing boundaries. Recognize your worth and value as you advocate for your needs and rights. Candace practiced self-appreciation, acknowledging her strength and resilience in prioritizing her well-being and honoring her values.

This structured approach to clarifying your deal breakers and establishing non-negotiable policies can cultivate a sense of empowerment and agency in your professional and personal life. Your boundaries will serve as a guiding compass, honoring your values and fostering healthy relationships and environments that support your growth and well-being.

7

PERSONAL GROWTH GOALS: SETTING RELATIONSHIP KPIS

As you've navigated the intricacies of navigating professional and personal landscapes, you've undoubtedly recognized the profound impact of setting goals. It's time to apply this principle to your relationships by establishing Personal Growth Goals and Relationship Key Performance Indicators (KPIs). Drawing upon the insights gained from earlier chapters and the experiences of individuals like Virginia, we'll outline a structured approach to cultivating personal growth within the context of your relationships.

Outline: Personal Growth Goals - Setting Relationship KPIs

1. Reflect on Your Relationship Dynamics

- Identify Strengths: Reflect on your relationship's strengths, acknowledging what has contributed to its growth and resilience. Consider moments of connection, communication, and mutual support. For example, let's revisit Virginia, who recognized the strength of her relationship's foundation in trust, respect, and shared values.

- Acknowledge Areas for Growth: Similarly, acknowledge areas within your relationship with room for improvement. Identify communication patterns, conflict resolution, or individual growth that could benefit from attention. Virginia identified opportunities for growth in fostering open communication and deeper emotional intimacy with her partner.

2. Define Personal Growth Goals

- Individual Development: Set personal growth goals that align with your values, aspirations, and areas of improvement. These goals should focus on your journey toward becoming the best version of yourself within the relationship. Virginia established goals for self-awareness, emotional expression, and personal fulfillment outside her partnership.

- Relationship Enhancement: Additionally, define goals that aim to enhance the quality and depth of your relationship. These goals should prioritize mutual growth, understanding, and connection with your partner. Virginia and her partner set goals to improve communication skills, cultivate shared interests, and support each other's dreams.

3. Establish Relationship KPIs

- Clear Metrics: Identify clear and measurable Key Performance Indicators (KPIs) that signify progress and success within your relationship. These KPIs should reflect your partnership goals' health, vitality, and alignment. Virginia and her partner established KPIs related to communication frequency, quality time spent together, and emotional attunement.

- Regular Evaluation: Regularly evaluate and track your Relationship KPIs to assess the effectiveness of your efforts and identify areas for adjustment or improvement. Use these evaluations as opportunities for open dialogue and shared reflection with your partner. Virginia and her partner scheduled regular check-ins to review their KPIs and discuss their relationship's trajectory.

4. Align Goals with Values and Vision

- Shared Values: Ensure that your Personal Growth Goals and Relationship KPIs align with your shared values and long-term vision as a couple. These goals should reflect your collective aspirations, principles, and priorities. Virginia and her partner ensured that their goals resonated with their shared values of trust, authenticity, and mutual support.

- Future Orientation: Keep your goals future-oriented, focusing on the growth and evolution of your relationship over time. Visualize the partnership you aspire to cultivate, and let that vision guide your goal-setting process. Virginia and her partner envisioned a relationship characterized by deep connection, shared purpose, and unwavering support for each other's growth.

5. Implement Action Plans

- Concrete Strategies: Develop concrete action plans to support achieving your Personal Growth Goals and Relationship KPIs. These plans should outline each goal's specific steps, timelines, and responsibilities. Virginia and her partner created action plans, including regular date nights, couples therapy sessions, and individual self-care practices.

- Accountability Measures: Establish accountability measures to ensure follow-through on your action plans and maintain momentum toward your goals. These measures may include regular progress updates, joint activities, or shared commitments. Virginia and her partner held each other accountable by scheduling weekly check-ins and celebrating milestones.

6. Embrace Flexibility and Adaptability

- Open Communication: Maintain open communication with your partner throughout your personal growth and relationship development journey. Be willing to adjust your goals and strategies based on changing circumstances or feedback. Virginia and her partner embraced open communication, regularly discussing their evolving needs, challenges, and aspirations.

- Adaptation: Cultivate adaptability as you navigate life and love's inevitable twists and turns. Be prepared to pivot your goals and action plans as needed, staying attuned to each other's needs and the dynamics of your relationship. Virginia and her partner remained flexible, adapting their goals and schedules to accommodate life's unpredictability while staying committed to their shared vision.

7. Celebrate Milestones and Achievements

- Recognition: Celebrate milestones and achievements in your personal growth and relationship journey, no matter how small. Take time to acknowledge progress, development, and moments of connection with your partner. Virginia and her partner celebrated improved communication, increased emotional intimacy, and successful conflict resolution.

- Gratitude: Practice gratitude for each other's efforts, support, and presence. Express appreciation for how you contribute to each other's growth and happiness. Virginia and her partner expressed gratitude regularly, affirming their love, commitment, and aspirations for the future.

Following this structured approach to setting Personal Growth Goals and Relationship KPIs, you can foster a relationship environment that supports mutual growth, understanding, and fulfillment. Your goals and KPIs will serve as guiding beacons, illuminating the path toward a more profound connection, shared purpose, and lasting love.

CONCLUSION:
INTEGRATING LOVE AND LABOR – THE PATH FORWARD

Reflecting on the profound insights gleaned from the intersections of love and labor is essential as we reach the culmination of our journey together. Throughout this exploration, we've delved into the depths of reclaiming our narratives, clarifying boundaries, and setting goals to foster personal and professional growth. Now, let's embark on the path forward, illuminated by the wisdom gained from our collective experiences.

1. Embracing Wholeness:

As we navigate the complexities of life, it's crucial to recognize that our professional and personal spheres are not disparate entities but interconnected facets of our existence. Just as our careers shape our identities, our relationships profoundly influence our well-being and fulfillment. By embracing the Wholeness of our beings, we unlock the potential for profound growth and harmony in both realms.

2. Honoring Resilience:

Our journey has underscored the remarkable resilience inherent within each of us. From facing layoffs and setbacks to navigating the intricacies of love and loss, we've demonstrated an unwavering capacity to adapt, evolve, and thrive in adversity.

Through these challenges, we forge the steel of our character and emerge more robust, more resilient beings.

3. Cultivating Authenticity:

Authenticity lies at the heart of our journey—a beacon guiding us toward genuine connections and meaningful endeavors. Embracing our true selves creates space for vulnerability, intimacy, and growth in our relationships and careers. Let us continue to cultivate authenticity as we navigate the complexities of love and labor, honoring our unique voices and experiences.

4. Nurturing Growth:

Growth is not merely a destination, but a continuous journey fueled by curiosity, courage, and self-reflection. As we move forward, let us commit to nurturing our personal and professional growth, setting intentions, and embracing the opportunities for learning and evolution each day brings. Through intentional action and self-discovery, we cultivate the seeds of our potential and blossom into our most whole selves.

5. Embracing Connection:

At the heart of our journey lies the profound power of connection to ourselves, others, and the world around us. As we navigate the intricacies of love and labor, let us cherish the connections we forge, drawing strength and inspiration from our bonds. In these connections, we find solace, support, and the courage to pursue our dreams.

6. Gratitude and Celebration:

Finally, let us pause to express gratitude for our shared journey and the growth we've experienced together. Let us celebrate our triumphs, no matter how small, and honor the lessons learned from our challenges. As we bid farewell to this chapter, let us carry forward a spirit of gratitude, resilience, and authenticity, illuminating the path ahead with the radiance of our shared experiences.

As we integrate the lessons of love and labor into our lives, may we continue to embrace the beauty of our journey—the highs and lows, the triumphs, and trials—with open hearts and unwavering courage. Through the alchemy of love and labor, we sculpt our destinies, weaving a tapestry of meaning, purpose, and fulfillment that transcends time and space. Onward, dear friends, to new horizons and boundless possibilities.

Made in the USA
Columbia, SC
10 December 2024